Inventions and Discoveries

Transportation

WORLD
BOOK

a Scott Fetzer company

Chicago

www.worldbookonline.com

World Book, Inc.
233 N. Michigan Avenue
Chicago, IL 60601
U.S.A.

For information about other World Book publications, visit our Web site at **http://www.worldbookonline.com** or call **1-800-WORLDBK (967-5325).**
For information about sales to schools and libraries, call **1-800-975-3250 (United States),** or **1-800-837-5365 (Canada).**

Editorial:
Editor in Chief: Paul A. Kobasa
Project Managers: Cassie Mayer, Michael Noren
Editor: Jake Bumgardner
Content Development: Odyssey Books
Writer: Brad Davies
Researcher: Cheryl Graham
**Manager, Contracts & Compliance
 (Rights & Permissions):** Loranne K. Shields
Indexer: David Pofelski

Graphics and Design:
Associate Director: Sandra M. Dyrlund
Manager, Graphics and Design: Tom Evans
Coordinator, Design Development and Production:
 Brenda B. Tropinski
Contributing Photographs Editor: Clover Morell
Senior Cartographer: John M. Rejba

Pre-Press and Manufacturing:
Director: Carma Fazio
Manufacturing Manager: Steven K. Hueppchen
Production/Technology Manager: Anne Fritzinger

Picture Acknowledgments:
Front Cover: © Natalia Bratslavsky, Shutterstock.
Back Cover: © Mary Evans Picture Library/Alamy Images.

© All Canada Photos/Alamy Images 7; © Jef Maion, Alamy Images 15; © Mary Evans Picture Library/Alamy Images 16, 27; AP/Wide World 19; Boeing Photo 29; © Alinari Archives/Corbis 35; © Corbis/Bettmann 15, 31, 33; General Electric 33; General Motors Corporation 26; © Car Culture/Getty Images 30; © Hulton Archive/Getty Images 17, 20, 29; © PatitucciPhoto/Getty Images 41; © Bill Pugliano, Getty Images 42; © Pete Seaward, Stone/Getty Images 5; Granger Collection 4, 8, 13, 17, 18, 22, 23, 24, 28; © H. Armstrong Roberts, ClassicStock/The Image Works 30; © SSPL/The Image Works 14; Mercedes-Benz 26; NASA 38, 39; Navstar 41; © Shutterstock 6, 7, 9, 10, 12, 13, 14, 21, 25, 27, 31, 32, 34, 36, 40, 44; Sikorsky Aircraft 34; U.S. National Air and Space Museum/Smithsonian Institution 28; Stock Montage 44.

All maps and illustrations are the exclusive property of World Book, Inc.

Library of Congress Cataloging-in-Publication Data

Transportation.
    p. cm. -- (Inventions and discoveries)
  Includes index.
  Summary: "An exploration of the transformative impact of inventions and discoveries in transportation. Features include fact boxes, sidebars, biographies, and a timeline, glossary, list of recommended reading and Web sites, and index"--Provided by publisher.
  ISBN 978-0-7166-0381-8
  1. Transportation--History--Juvenile literature. 2. Transportation--United States--History--Juvenile literature. I. World Book, Inc.
HE152.T67 2009
388--dc22
                  2008040629

Inventions and Discoveries
Set ISBN: 978-0-7166-0380-1
Printed in China
1 2 3 4 5 12 11 10 09

▶ Table of Contents

There is a glossary of terms on pages 45-46. Terms defined in the glossary are in type **that looks like this** on their first appearance on any spread (two facing pages).

What is an invention?

An invention is a new device, new product, or new way of doing something. Inventions change the way we live. Before the car was invented, some people rode horses to travel long distances. Before the light bulb was invented, people used candles and similar sources of light to see at night. The invention of farming allowed people to stay in one place instead of wandering in search of food. As people established villages and invented ways to travel to other villages, trade (the exchange of goods) flourished. Technological advances soon produced a great variety of new goods, services, and capabilities. Today, inventions continue to shape people's lives every day.

For much of human history, people used animal-drawn vehicles to travel long distances over land.

What is transportation?

Transportation is the process of moving people and things from one place to another. People use transportation to go where they need to go and to get the things they want or need. Without transportation, there could be no trade, and towns and cities could not develop. Without transportation, **civilization** could not exist as it does today.

In prehistoric times, people traveled on foot. Shelter and supplies had to be carried on their backs or dragged along on sledges (heavy sleds). In time, people began to use animals, wagons, and boats to carry things. Thousands of years later, engine-powered vehicles marked the beginning of a revolution in transportation. Travel soon became faster and more convenient.

Today, people all over the world travel daily in cars and trucks, on trains and boats, and on airplanes. Advances in transportation have even made it possible for human beings to visit the moon and explore outer space.

Modern transportation takes many forms, as seen here in the busy streets of Tokyo, Japan.

The Wheel

Wheels, like many early tools, were sometimes made of stone.

For many years, people traveled on foot and carried their belongings on their backs. Around 5000 B.C. (about 7,000 years ago), people began using such animals as donkeys and oxen to carry things. Then, about 1,500 years later, the wheel appeared. The wheel is one of the most important inventions in history.

The wheel was probably invented in Mesopotamia (a region in the Middle East) between 3500 and 3000 B.C. The invention helped make Mesopotamia one of the world's first great **civilizations.** Because the wheel made it easier for people to travel and carry goods, trade expanded and life improved.

The first wheels were made from single, flat planks (pieces of wood) that were cut to form circles. But large planks required large trees, which were harder to find than small trees. So early wheel makers developed a method of attaching three smaller pieces of wood together to make wheels.

Use of the wheel spread quickly through most of Europe and central Asia. Within 1000 years, the wheel had rolled its way into China and India. After the invention of the wheel, people soon developed carts and wagons. These devices enabled people to carry things like grain over greater distances. Donkey-drawn carts even carried Mesopotamian soldiers into battle.

Many early wheels, as on this oxcart, were made from pieces of solid wood.

Early carts and wagons had two or four wheels and were pulled by oxen or donkeys. They bumped along slowly and probably needed repairs often. Horses were not used to pull these carts, because early harnesses made it difficult for the horses to breathe when the load was heavy.

The first wheels with **spokes** appeared in Egypt between 2000 and 1500 B.C. Spoked wheels were lighter than solid wheels, so it became possible for animals, such as horses, to pull carts faster over longer distances. The earliest spoked wheels were probably made for lightweight horse-drawn vehicles called **chariots,** the fastest vehicles of ancient times.

Today, the wheel is more important than ever. Cars, trucks, airplanes, and trains all use wheels to carry people and goods around the world. The advanced wheels and tires of today work exactly the same way as the wooden wheels did thousands of years ago.

Modern tires are often made of rubber and filled with air.

A CLOSER LOOK

Why is trade important? People cannot make or grow everything they want and need. Through trade, people obtain the things that they do not have but can get from others. Trade allows people to share different inventions and ideas with one another.

How important were wheeled carts? With wheeled carts, food and other items could be moved in large quantities. Carts carried objects too heavy or too large for people to carry otherwise. In ancient times, carts were considered so important that they were buried with important people as a sign of honor.

Spoked wheels are lighter and allow faster speeds than solid wheels.

▶ The Sail

In ancient Egypt, the most advanced boats were long, narrow vessels powered by rows of people paddling with oars. These boats, called galleys, were built mainly for travel along the Nile River. By about 3000 B.C., the use of wind power expanded boat travel from rivers to the sea. The invention of the sail enabled people to travel across oceans to spread new ideas, inventions, and ways of life. Busy port cities soon grew into major cultural centers.

The first sails were square, and they were attached to a single mast (tall central pole that holds the sail upright). However, rowers were still needed when there was no wind.

Around 1200 B.C., the Phoenicians (*fuh NIHSH uhns*) and Greeks designed ships that used multiple sails of different shapes. By 300 B.C., four-sail Greek ships regularly carried passengers and **cargo** from Egypt to Rome. These ships had both square and triangular sails. Square sails work well with winds blowing from behind, but triangular sails, called lateens, work well even when sailing into the wind.

From the late A.D. 700's to about 1100, Viking ships with teams of rowers and square sails were the best ships in northern Europe. Vikings sailed their famous longships across the North Atlantic Ocean to Greenland and North America. Leif Eriksson, a Viking explorer, landed in North America about 500 years before Christopher Columbus arrived there in 1492.

In the mid-1400's, ships with three masts and both square and triangular sails were used by great ex-

Vikings sailed longships like this one across the North Atlantic Ocean.

Christopher Columbus sailed in ships with both square and triangular sails.

plorers, such as Christopher Columbus and Ferdinand Magellan.

By the mid-1500's, galleons—large, fast ships armed with cannons—sailed the seas. During the 1600's, trading ships called East Indiamen carried silk, spices, ivory, and other goods from India, China, and the East Indies to Europe. By the early 1800's, people and goods traveled regularly between Europe and the United States on large sailing ships.

By the early 1900's, steam-powered ships had replaced sailing ships as the chief vessels used in trade. The world quickly became smaller, as steamships could cross the seas much more quickly than sailing ships could. Still, sailing ships remain widely used in sport and recreation.

Today, giant container ships carry cargo all around the world.

▶ The Sternpost Rudder

The sternpost rudder made it easier for people to steer large sailing ships.

In ancient times, people directed ships by moving steering oars.

Sternpost rudder

By A.D. 1200, people had been using ships for trade for thousands of years. However, crossing the seas was dangerous, and trade routes were confined to rivers and coastal waters. Shipbuilders worked to design stronger ships, but the ships' movement and safety at sea were limited.

Dating back to ancient Egypt, people directed ships by moving large oars near the stern (back) of the ves-

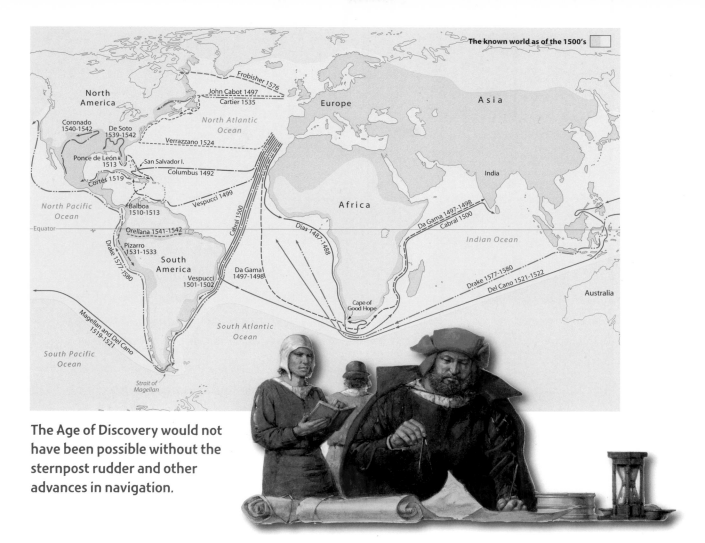

The known world as of the 1500's

North America

Frobisher 1576
John Cabot 1497
Cartier 1535

Coronado 1540-1542
De Soto 1539-1542

Verrazzano 1524

Ponce de León 1513
San Salvador I.
Cortés 1519
Columbus 1492

North Atlantic Ocean

Europe

Asia

India

North Pacific Ocean

Balboa 1510-1513

Vespucci 1499

Africa

Da Gama 1497-1498
Cabral 1500

Equator

Orellana 1541-1542

Cabral 1500

Dias 1487-1488

Indian Ocean

Pizarro 1531-1533

Drake 1577-1580

South America

Da Gama 1497-1498

Drake 1577-1580
Del Cano 1521-1522

Australia

Vespucci 1501-1502

Cape of Good Hope

Magellan and Del Cano 1519-1521

South Atlantic Ocean

South Pacific Ocean

Strait of Magellan

The Age of Discovery would not have been possible without the sternpost rudder and other advances in navigation.

sel. These oars worked as rudders—flat, movable pieces used for steering. However, the oars did not work well on large ships or in rough water, and they often broke during storms. The use of oars as rudders curbed how far from land people could safely sail.

Then came the invention of the sternpost rudder—a piece of wood or metal connected to a long upright post in the back of the boat. The post extends from the ship's deck into the water beneath the stern. Different types of sternpost rudders were in-

vented in China, Persia, and Europe. They all allowed for larger, stronger ships that people could steer more easily.

With a sternpost rudder, ships could sail through rough seas and venture farther from land. The sternpost rudder, combined with the invention of the **compass** and other navigation tools, helped revolutionize travel by sea. These developments led to the Age of Discovery, a period of great European exploration that began in the 1400's.

▶ The Stirrup

Stirrups are made specially to support a rider's feet.

As early as 5,000 years ago, people used horses to make transportation faster and easier. These early riders used horses while hunting for food or going into battle. People also used horses to pull carts, wagons, and plows. Horses could carry large amounts of food and supplies on their backs.

For many years, however, balancing on a horse's back was difficult. It was especially tricky when the rider was also trying to throw a spear or swing a sword while riding. As a result, horseback riding was limited in warfare and in certain other areas of

life. This changed with the invention of the **stirrup.**

The stirrup was a simple but very important invention. A stirrup is usually a loop of metal or wood that hangs from the side of a saddle to support the rider's foot. Riders with stirrups on their feet are much more stable and can travel with greater speed.

Stirrups came from China to India and then to Europe in the A.D. 400's. With the arrival of the stirrup, mounted (on horseback) warriors called knights became more important in warfare. The English soon began to breed large, powerful warhorses that could carry a man wearing a heavy suit of armor.

The stirrup also played an important role in the development and exploration of North America. Spanish explorers rode horses as they traveled across new lands. American pioneers who settled the West also rode horses. Mounted soldiers fought in the American Revolution (1775-1783) and the American Civil War (1861-1865). Riders on horseback

Mounted riders became faster with the use of stirrups.

also served as the fastest method of long-distance communication until the telegraph enabled people to send messages over wires.

Today, the horse is not as important for transportation as it once was. However, people still use horses for recreation, sport, and work. Children and adults ride horses for fun and exercise. Large crowds thrill to the excitement of horse races. Horses also perform in circuses, rodeos, carnivals, parades, and horse shows. They help ranchers round up cattle and are sometimes ridden by soldiers and police officers.

Stirrups help riders stay in the saddle.

This old mariner's compass consists of a compass card in a wooden bowl.

In ancient times, sailors navigated by observing the sun and stars and by studying the seasonal directions of the wind. But these basic methods of navigation were unreliable for great distances, especially in bad weather. As a result, sea travelers usually stayed safely within sight of land.

More than 2,000 years ago, the Chinese developed one of the most significant navigation tools ever invented—the **magnetic compass.** This device uses Earth's **magnetic field** to indicate direction.

The first compasses were simple pieces of magnetic iron, usually floated on straw or cork in a bowl of water. Earth's magnetic field would cause the piece of iron to point roughly toward the North Pole. Later compass designs looked more like clocks. These designs have a rotating magnetic needle and a surface called a compass card. The compass card is labeled with letters that stand for the four directions—north, south, east, and west. These are called the **cardinal points** of a compass.

The modern mariner's compass still uses a floating compass card.

Magnetic compasses on boats and ships are called mariner's compasses. In most mariner's compasses, the magnetic needle is attached to the underside of the compass card. This means that the entire card rotates, with the point labeled N (for north) always pointing toward the North Pole.

Chinese and Mediterranean navigators first used the magnetic compass to guide their ships around the A.D. 1000's or 1100's. Over time, the device enabled sea travelers to stray far from land and to keep from getting lost, even in the middle of the ocean. With improved sense of direction, explorers increasingly traveled from one continent to another to trade, explore, gain territory, or spread religion.

Today, ships and airplanes continue to use compasses for their travels across the globe. In addition, hikers often carry compasses as they explore unfamiliar places.

Compasses help hikers find their way in unfamiliar places.

The Horse and Carriage

This ancient Syrian chariot is armed and ready for battle.

During the **Middle Ages** (about the 400's through the 1400's), wagon rides could be extremely bumpy. Roads were usually in bad shape, and most wagons had no suspension systems (shock absorbers, springs, or similar devices) to cushion the ride. By the 1600's, horse-drawn wagons hauled goods locally, but they were rarely used for long trips or personal transportation. Most people still traveled on foot or horseback.

In the early 1700's, the carriage was developed. Carriages were lighter and more graceful than the heavy wagons and coaches that had been used in the past. The carriage's **running gear** was usually made of strong, springy wood like oak, ash, or hickory. Early carriage wheels were usually made of hickory and fitted with iron tires. Solid rubber tires came into use after 1875.

Along with the development of the carriage, France and Britain created

> **FUN FACT** The first well-built roads were made by the Romans in the A.D. 100's and 200's. The roads helped the Romans rule their huge empire, which included, at its peak, about half of Europe, much of the Middle East, and the north coast of Africa.

the first well-built paved roads since ancient **Roman** times (27 B.C. to A.D. 395). Better roads permitted the use of faster carriages.

Carriages were first brought to the American Colonies from England and France. By 1880, the United States produced more horse-drawn vehicles than any other country in the world. Popular American carriages went by names like the buckboard, the buggy, the chaise, and the rockaway. People of wealth and social standing used fashionable carriages called landaus and victorias. Other types of carriages included ambulances, buses, hackneys (taxis), hearses, limousines, sleighs, and classic **stagecoaches.**

The use of carriages peaked in 1905, when U.S. builders produced more than 930,000 carriages. However, the introduction of the automo-

bile—sometimes called the "horseless carriage"—soon brought an end to the age of the horse-drawn vehicle. By World War I (1914-1918), carriage use had declined significantly.

Today, some people still use carriages. They are especially popular among tourists in major cities.

In 1905, people took the stagecoach down Fifth Avenue in New York City.

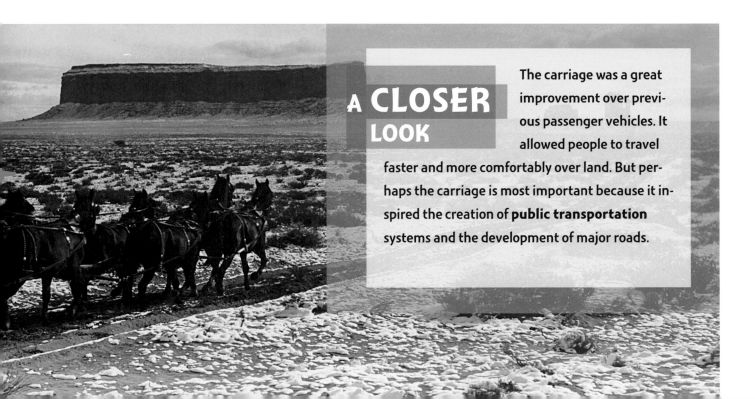

A CLOSER LOOK

The carriage was a great improvement over previous passenger vehicles. It allowed people to travel faster and more comfortably over land. But perhaps the carriage is most important because it inspired the creation of **public transportation** systems and the development of major roads.

The Balloon

A Montgolfier balloon rises over the city of Paris in 1864.

In 1782, two French brothers named Joseph and Jacques Montgolfier (*mont GAHL fee uhr*) found that filling small paper bags with smoke caused the bags to rise. This discovery led to the beginning of balloon transportation.

In June of 1783, the Montgolfier brothers sent up a large smoke-filled balloon at a public gathering in Annonay, France. Three months later, France's King Louis XVI looked on as they launched a balloon carrying a sheep, a duck, and a rooster.

In October 1783, the French scientist Jean F. Pilâtre de Rozier became the first person to go up in a balloon. He floated about 80 feet (24 meters) in the air in a Montgolfier balloon that was tied to the ground. The next month, he and a French nobleman, the Marquis (*mar KEE*) d'Arlandes, made the first **free flight.** The balloon, built by the Montgolfier brothers, carried the two men about 5 miles (8 kilometers) across Paris.

Around the same time, a French chemist named Jacques Alexandre Charles worked on balloons filled with hydrogen gas, which is lighter than air. The first hydrogen balloon was launched in Paris in August 1783. The first human flight in a hydrogen balloon took place in December of that year.

The first practical use of balloons was in warfare. In 1794, France used balloons anchored to the ground as observation platforms during conflicts with other European nations. The balloons enabled the French to learn the

A **CLOSER**
LOOK

One of the most famous airships in history was the *Hindenburg*. It provided the first commercial passenger air service across the Atlantic Ocean. Sadly, the *Hindenburg* is best remembered for exploding in 1937 after the flammable hydrogen gas inside the craft ignited. The explosion killed 35 of the 97 people on board. The *Hindenburg* disaster ended regular passenger service on airships.

locations of enemy troops and to direct the movement of their own troops. Balloons were used for similar purposes in later wars. During World War I (1914-1918) and World War II (1939-1945), some balloons also dropped bombs.

Early balloons led to the invention of **airships.** These huge, cigar-shaped balloons were filled with lighter-than-air gas and had engines and propellers to move them through the air. They also could be steered by a pilot. These airships provided regular passenger service during the early 1900's.

Today, large balloons are used mostly for scientific research—particularly for studies of the weather—and for recreation.

Balloons like this one help meteorologists (weather scientists) forecast the weather.

The Steam Locomotive

An English locomotive hauls three carriages in 1845.

Around 1800, the English inventor Richard Trevithick mounted a **steam engine** on a four-wheeled vehicle designed to roll along a track. In 1804, he used this vehicle to pull 10 tons (9 metric tons) of iron, 70 men, and 5 wagons along 9 miles (15 kilometers) of track. Trevithick had invented the world's first successful railroad **locomotive.**

In the early 1800's, a few horse-powered railroads began operating in the eastern United States. In fact, the first railroad cars to carry passengers in the United States were pulled by horses. But in 1830, a steam locomotive called the *Best Friend of Charleston* made the first run of a steam-powered train in the United States. In 1831, the South Carolina Canal and Railroad Company became the first U.S. railroad to provide regular steam-powered passenger and **cargo** service.

Railroad building spread rapidly, first in the United Kingdom, and then throughout Europe and the rest of the world. By 1870, most of Europe's major rail systems had been built. The first transcontinental (crossing a continent) railroad across the United States was finished in 1869. By the turn of the century, the United States had five transcontinental rail lines.

When water boils and turns to steam, it expands. This expanding steam can be used to power an engine by turning a **turbine** or pushing **pistons**. The development of the steam engine in the 1700's made modern industry possible. Until then, people had to depend on the power of their own muscles or on animal, wind, or water power.

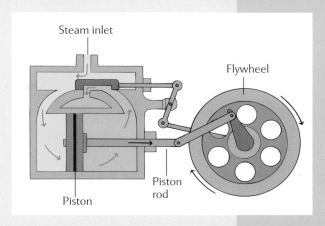

The completion of these railroads opened large regions of North America to town development, farming, and trade. By 1900, steam locomotives transported 80 to 90 percent of the people and cargo traveling between U.S. cities.

In the late 1800's, France, Germany, and the United Kingdom built railroads in their colonies (lands they controlled) in Africa and Asia. The United Kingdom also helped build nearly 25,000 miles (40,200 kilometers) of railroad track in India around this time.

Argentina and Brazil developed rapidly after they built large rail networks (interconnected systems) in the late 1800's. In 1916, Russia completed its 5,600-mile (9,000-kilometer) Trans-Siberian railroad. The Trans-Siberian is the world's longest continuous railroad.

Today, nearly every country uses railroads. And although steam locomotives have mostly been replaced with modern **diesel** and electric locomotives, the importance of the train remains. Every day, thousands of trains carry goods and passengers along tracks throughout the world.

This freight train carries goods across the beautiful Canadian landscape.

▶ The Steamboat

Steamboats puff their way down the Ohio River in 1911.

In 1787, an inventor named John Fitch demonstrated the first working **steamboat** in the United States. His 45-foot (14-meter) boat was powered by a **steam engine** and paddle wheels (side-mounted wheels with paddles around them). It reached a speed of about 3 miles (5 kilometers) per hour on the Delaware River. Fitch later developed a steamboat for passenger and **freight** service, but he lacked enough money to keep operating.

The first steamboat to be commercially successful (successful in business) was the *Clermont*, built by the American inventor and artist Robert Fulton. The boat first traveled up the Hudson River from New York City to Albany, New York, in August 1807.

Soon, the *Clermont* was carrying passengers regularly. In 1809, Fulton joined with another inventor, Nicholas Roosevelt, to produce steamboats to operate on western rivers, such as the Ohio and the Mississippi.

While Fulton's boats were traveling on bays and rivers, the American **engineer** John Stevens was building a steamship named the *Phoenix*. When the *Phoenix* steamed along the Atlantic coast in 1809, it became the first steam-driven vessel to make an ocean voyage.

In 1819, an American vessel called the *Savannah* became the first steamship to cross the Atlantic

Ocean. But the *Savannah* was actually a sailing ship with steam-powered paddle wheels. In 1838, a British ship named *Sirius* became the first ship to offer regularly scheduled service across the Atlantic using steam power alone.

Over time, new types of engines and new sources of power developed. Ships were built of steel rather than wood. Paddle wheels largely gave way to **propellers.** By the early 1900's, large, fast, comfortable passenger ships called luxury liners began crossing the Atlantic. One of the most famous of these ships was the *Mauretania,* a British vessel launched in 1907.

Before long, steamships were being replaced by ships powered by **diesel** engines and even by **nuclear power.** Still, steamships remain in use in many parts of the world today, often as popular tourist attractions.

Robert Fulton

Robert Fulton (1765-1815) was an American inventor, engineer, and artist. He was born on a farm in Pennsylvania. As a boy, he made his own lead pencils, household utensils for his mother, and even skyrockets for a town celebration. In his teenage years, Fulton worked for a jeweler and gained fame as a painter.

In 1807, Fulton brought in a new era in transportation when he introduced the *Clermont,* the first commercially successful steamboat. Among Fulton's other inventions were a machine for making rope and a machine for cutting canals (waterways dug across land for ship and boat travel). Fulton also experimented with submarine design.

Robert Fulton's steamboat, the *Clermont,* navigates the Hudson River in 1813.

▶ The Bicycle

The draisine looked like a bicycle but had no pedals.

The first direct ancestor to the bicycle was the **draisine,** invented in 1817 by Baron Karl von Drais of Germany. To operate a draisine, a person sat on a frame between two wheels, pushed off the ground, and steered with the front wheel. Nicknamed the "hobby horse," this foot-propelled vehicle was made entirely of wood and had no pedals. In 1839, the Scottish blacksmith Kirkpatrick Macmillan added pedals to the draisine and, in the process, created the first true bicycle.

Different versions of the bicycle became popular in the 1860's. Most had pedals attached directly to the front wheel. These early bicycles were called "bone shakers" due to the extremely bumpy ride along the cobblestone streets of the day.

Around 1870, a new type of bicycle called the **high-wheeler** appeared. High-wheelers had a huge front wheel and a small rear wheel. The tires were solid iron or rubber. Each turn of the pedals turned the

Kirkpatrick Macmillan added pedals to the draisine (left) in 1839. Pierre Lallement brought his bicycle (right) to the United States in 1866.

With the high-wheeler (left), accidents were common. Luckily, the safety bike (right) appeared before too long.

front wheel around once, so the bike traveled a long distance with a single turn of the pedals. But with the large front wheel, accidents were common.

Around 1885, the safety bike appeared. Its wheels were the same size, so it was easier and safer to ride than a high-wheeler. The safety bike also had a **chain-and-sprocket system,** like modern bikes. With this system, pedal rotations move a chain that causes the rear wheel to turn.

By 1890, bicycles were being made with adjustable handlebars and coaster brakes (brakes operated by pushing backward on the pedals). They also had air-filled rubber tires, which made for a smoother ride.

The interest in bicycles declined after the automobile became popular in the early 1900's. But bikes regained importance in the late 1900's, as more people rode them for fun, ex-

ercise, and sport. Popular bicycle sports include track racing, road racing, **BMX** (bicycle motocross), and mountain biking.

Today, many people use bicycles for everyday transportation. When people ride bikes instead of driving cars, it helps reduce air **pollution.** Many city streets now have special bicycle lanes.

Every summer, cyclists compete in the *Tour de France*, the biggest bike race in the world.

► The Automobile

The Cugnot steam tractor of 1769 rolled along at a speed of less than 2 miles (3 kilometers) per hour.

Beginning in the late 1700's, a number of **engineers** experimented with steam-powered automobiles. However, the steam cars had many disadvantages, and they eventually disappeared. The automobile as we know it today resulted from the development of the **internal-combustion engine.**

An internal-combustion engine burns a mixture of fuel and air. The first engine of this type was created in 1860 by a Belgian man named Jean Joseph Étienne Lenoir (*luh NWAHR*). At first, Lenoir's engines powered things like printing presses and water pumps. But in 1885, two German inventors, Gottlieb Daimler (*DYM luhr*) and Karl Benz, built gasoline-powered engines that could be used in cars. Other inventors soon followed, and the automobile **industry** was born.

In 1897, Ransom E. Olds started the Olds Motor Vehicle Company in Detroit, Michigan. The company created the first **assembly line** and became the first mass producer of gasoline-powered automobiles in the

Karl Benz put a gasoline engine in his *Motorwagen* (left). A few years later, Ransom E. Olds drove his car (right) up the steps of the Michigan Capitol.

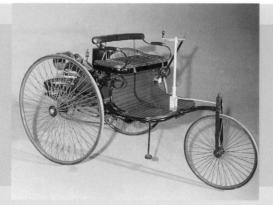

1885 Benz

1901 Oldsmobile

Henry Ford

Henry Ford (1863–1947) was born in Michigan and grew up to become an engineer at an electric company. He built his first gasoline engine in 1893. In 1896, he built a car.

In 1903, Henry Ford started the Ford Motor Company. Ford improved the idea of the assembly line, where parts were carried to workers on a moving belt. Each worker did only one job. This method shortened the time it took to make a car and made them cheaper. By 1924, the price of a Model T had dropped from $850 to $260.

United States. By 1903, Olds was competing with other car companies like Cadillac, Buick, and Ford. By 1908, Henry Ford had created the Model T, an affordable, reliable car. By 1914, Ford was producing half of the cars made in the United States.

As cars became more popular, they changed the way people lived. People gained greater freedom to decide where they wanted to go and when. Workers with cars could now live farther from their jobs, so many families moved outside cities to towns called **suburbs.** Farmers with cars or trucks could sell their crops in more distant places.

As more and more cars traveled streets around the world, a number of new challenges emerged. For instance, oil is needed to produce gasoline. Most countries do not produce enough oil to meet their needs. In addition, cars give off harmful fumes that cause **pollution.**

To address these concerns, automobile makers are working to develop cars that use less fuel and create less pollution. They are also developing cars that run on alternative (different) fuels, such as electricity and hydrogen.

Cars crowd busy streets in Chicago, Illinois, on a summer afternoon.

▶ The Airplane

Many inventors experimented with gliders during the 1800's.

In 1804, a British inventor named Sir George Cayley built the first successful **glider.** It resembled an airplane, but it was small, had no engine, and flew without a passenger. Cayley later built full-sized gliders capable of carrying a person.

Over the next 100 years, people tried to attach engines and **propellers** to gliders to achieve powered flight. Some inventors came close, but none of these early machines flew successfully. In the 1890's, an American scientist named Samuel P. Langley built a steam-powered model airplane that flew for more than half a mile (nearly a kilometer). However, his tests of a larger, passenger-carrying version were unsuccessful.

In 1899, two American brothers named Orville and Wilbur Wright started building gliders. After many experiments, they developed a way to control an aircraft while in flight. In 1903, they built a double-winged airplane called a biplane. The plane, named the *Flyer*, was powered by a lightweight gasoline engine and two propellers. On December 17, 1903,

Orville Wright piloted an airplane around the top of the Statue of Liberty in 1909.

Orville Wright successfully flew this plane near Kitty Hawk, North Carolina.

After the success of the Wright brothers, pilots and inventors worked continuously to improve airplane design. At the start of World War I (1914-1918), the airplane was still a novelty. However, the demands of warfare led to many new improvements over a short period of time. By the end of the war, many airplanes could go 130 miles (209 kilometers) per hour or faster.

In the 1920's and 1930's, such pilots as Charles Lindbergh and Amelia Earhart became world-famous for their daring long-distance and high-altitude flights. Airplane development improved, and commercial aviation became popular. By 1938, more than a million Americans were flying every year.

World War II (1939-1945) again saw rapid development in flight technology. By the late 1950's, passenger planes with **jet engines** were flying virtually everywhere in the world.

Today, hundreds of thousands of airplanes are in use all around the globe. Planes are the fastest practical way to transport passengers and **cargo** over great distances. They carry out missions for the military, help fight forest fires, and deliver emergency aid to people in need.

The Wright Brothers

The Wright brothers, Orville (1871-1948) and Wilbur (1867-1912), invented and built the first successful airplane. Orville, pictured at the left, was born in Dayton, Ohio, and Wilbur, at the right, was born in Millville, Indiana. As children they sold homemade mechanical toys.

As a young man, Orville built his own printing press. The brothers launched a weekly paper in Dayton, the *West Side News*, with Wilbur as editor. They also began to rent, sell, and make bicycles.

The Wright brothers began experimenting with aircraft, eventually creating a two-winged plane named the *Flyer*. On December 17, 1903, they made the world's first powered flight near Kitty Hawk, North Carolina.

Large commercial airliners bring distant parts of the world within easy reach of one another.

► The Electric Starter

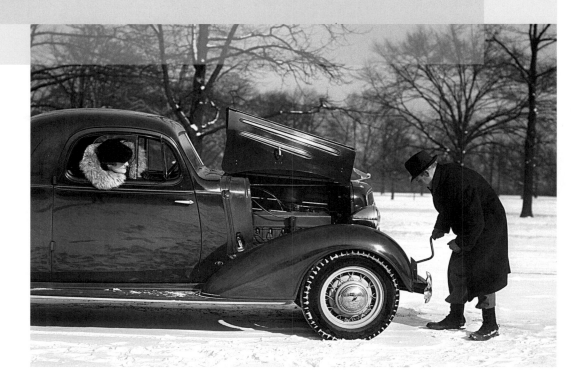

Electric starters eventually eliminated the task of starting cars with a hand crank.

The 1912 Cadillac was the first car with an electric starter.

A campfire needs to be lit with a match before it can burn. In the same way, an **internal-combustion engine** needs a starter—a device that sets the engine in motion.

In the earliest automobiles, a person would insert a large crank into the front of the engine and turn the crank by hand. The crank turned a part called the crankshaft, which would spin as the engine started. Hand cranking was difficult, troublesome, and sometimes dangerous. After the engine started, the crank was supposed to come out of the crankshaft. However, sometimes the crank would not come out, and the spinning crank would injure the person starting the car.

An American **engineer** named Charles Kettering invented the first useful electric self-starter in 1911.

When the driver turns the key in the car's ignition, an **electric current** flows to the battery. Then an electric current flows from the battery to the starting motor, which cranks the engine.

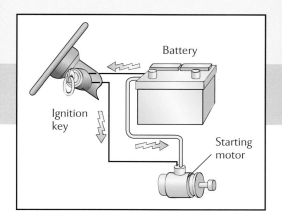

The starter made it possible to start an engine without using a crank. Kettering's invention was a major development in automobile design. It made starting car engines safer, easier, and more convenient.

The American company General Motors first installed electric starters in its 1912 Cadillacs. By 1920, most automobiles had done away with hand crank starters.

Some of the earliest electric starters were made with a button inside the car that the driver could push to start the engine. In most modern automobiles, the driver turns a key in the ignition to make the engine run.

Charles Kettering poses with his electric self-starter.

A key begins the starting process in most modern cars.

The Jet Engine

Turbofan jet engines run more quietly and use less fuel than other types of jet engines.

Around A.D. 60, an Egyptian scientist named Hero built a small toy-like device that may have been the first **jet engine.** His device was a hollow sphere (ball) with two nozzles sticking out in opposite directions. When water was heated inside the sphere, the steam escaping through the nozzles caused the device to spin. Almost 1,900 years later, jet engines, based on the same principles as Hero's sphere, would begin to power aircraft.

At the start of World War II (1939-1945), various countries sought to increase their military strength through air power. Scientists knew that jet-powered aircraft would be able to fly faster and higher than **propeller**-driven airplanes. As a result, several countries raced to produce the first practical jet aircraft.

In 1939, Germany made the first successful jet plane flight. The aircraft used a type of engine called a **turbojet,** designed by Hans von Ohain. In 1940, another jet-powered airplane was built and flown in Italy. However, neither of these jet engines was fully practical.

By 1941, Frank Whittle, an officer in the United Kingdom's Royal Air Force, had developed a more successful turbojet engine. But Germany created the first successful jet fighter, the Messerschmitt Me262. It flew combat missions toward the end of the war.

During the late 1940's, **engineers** worked to improve the jet engines built during World War II. By the early 1950's, the United States and the Soviet Union had highly effective military jets. By the mid-1950's, U.S. engineers were also designing com-

Jet propulsion is the production of motion in one direction by the release of a high-pressure stream of gas in the opposite direction. As air enters a jet engine, it is compressed (squeezed together), mixed with fuel, and burned. A fast-moving gas then shoots out the rear of the engine, causing the engine to move forward.

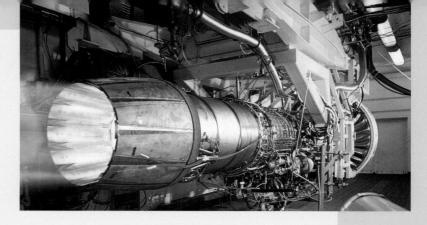

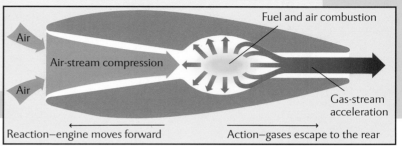

Fuel and air combustion

Air

Air-stream compression

Air

Gas-stream acceleration

Reaction—engine moves forward

Action—gases escape to the rear

mercial jet airliners. Propeller-driven aircraft became increasingly rare, as jet engines became standard for all types of planes—military, private, and commercial.

Modern airliners use **turbofan** engines. A turbofan is a variation of the turbojet that uses part of its power to turn a large fan. Today, researchers continue their efforts to increase the efficiency of jet engines and to reduce the **pollution** they produce.

Charles Yeager

Charles (Chuck) Yeager (1923-   ) was the first person to fly an aircraft faster than the speed of sound. At sea level, the speed of sound is about 770 miles (1,235 kilometers) per hour. He achieved this speed in a Bell X-1 rocket airplane on October 14, 1947. He set another record on December 12, 1953, by flying 2 ½ times the speed of sound in a Bell X-1A.

Yeager was born in Myra, West Virginia. During World War II (1939-1945), he served as a fighter pilot. In 1975, he retired from the military with the rank of brigadier general.

► The Helicopter

Igor Sikorsky first flew his single-rotor helicopter in 1939.

In 1483, the great Italian artist and scientist Leonardo da Vinci sketched a design for a helicopter. However, it would be hundreds of years before one got off the ground.

A helicopter is lifted into the air by spinning wings called **rotors.** Helicopters can fly forward, backward, sideways, or straight up and down. They can even hover (stay in one spot in the air). Helicopters can also lift off and land in small places, unlike air-planes, which require a long runway.

Throughout the 1800's, inventors experimented with model helicopters but were unable to build one at full size. They had more success in the early 1900's, as small, powerful gasoline engines became available. With these engines, inventors were finally able to build helicopters large enough to lift a person.

In 1907, the French inventor Louis Breguet demonstrated a helicopter that could lift an assistant about 2 feet (60 centimeters) into the air. The helicopter was unsteady, however,

F U N **F A C T** Helicopters are known by many nicknames, including *choppers, eggbeaters,* and *whirlybirds.*

and had to be held as it hovered. Later in 1907, a French mechanic named Paul Cornu made the first free flight in a helicopter. He flew his aircraft to a height of about 6 feet (1.8 meters) for about 20 seconds.

Improvements in helicopter design continued over the following decades. In 1936, a German inventor named Henrich Focke built a helicopter that reached a speed of 76 miles (122 kilometers) per hour and an altitude of 8,000 feet (2,400 meters). It stayed in the air for 80 minutes.

The earliest helicopters were designed with two or more rotors. Today, single-rotor helicopters are more common. The first flight of a practical single-rotor helicopter took place in the United States in 1939. The craft was built and flown by Igor

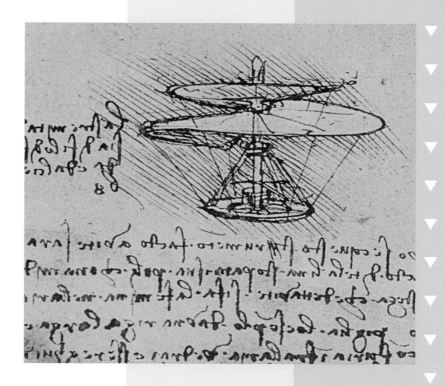

Sikorsky, a Russian **engineer** living in the United States. British and U.S. armed forces used an improved version of Sikorsky's helicopter during World War II (1939-1945).

Today, helicopters are used for a variety of purposes. Their ability to hover makes them especially useful for rescue missions. Police helicopters chase criminals and direct squad cars. Farmers use helicopters to spread fertilizers (substances that help plants grow). Radio and television stations use helicopters to report news stories and check traffic.

Leonardo da Vinci's sketches show a flying machine similar to a helicopter.

Military helicopters can serve as flying ambulances or troop transports.

▶ The Maglev Train

This maglev train in Shanghai, China, takes its passengers 19 miles in just 7 minutes.

Growing concerns over fuel supply and **pollution** have led scientists around the world to look for more efficient and cleaner forms of transportation. Inventors continuously search for fuels that are plentiful and less harmful to the environment. And as more and more people use public transportation, the need for fuel-efficient trains is greater than ever.

Over the past 40 years, several countries have developed **magnetic levitation trains,** or maglev trains. A maglev train is a vehicle that uses magnetic forces to float above a fixed track, called a guideway, without touching it. Because the train floats above the guideway, its speed is not limited by **friction** or vibration.

There are two important types of maglev technology: electrodynamic and electromagnetic. Electrodynamic maglev uses magnetic repulsion (pushing away) to make the train float. Electromagnetic maglev uses magnetic attraction.

Japanese researchers have developed electrodynamic maglev test vehicles that travel at speeds of up to 340 miles (550 kilometers) per hour. The Japanese design is based on magnet research done in the 1960's by the U.S. scientists James R. Powell and Gordon T. Danby.

A group of German companies began to develop a series of electro-magnetic maglev test vehicles in the early 1970's. German researchers have tested full-sized trains that can run as fast as 310 miles (499 kilometers) per hour.

From 1984 to 1995, a low-speed maglev operated as an airport shuttle in Birmingham, England. In 2004, commercial service began on a German-designed system that operates in China. These trains have reached speeds of up to 270 miles (430 kilometers) per hour.

Maglev train systems are extremely expensive to build, and scientists are not certain of how they might react to different city environments. As a result, few maglev trains have ever been built.

Still, maglev trains have a number of significant advantages over wheeled trains. They can reach higher speeds and operate more smoothly and quietly. Their guideways, which are usually elevated, require little maintenance. Also, they use **electric current** for power, so they produce little pollution.

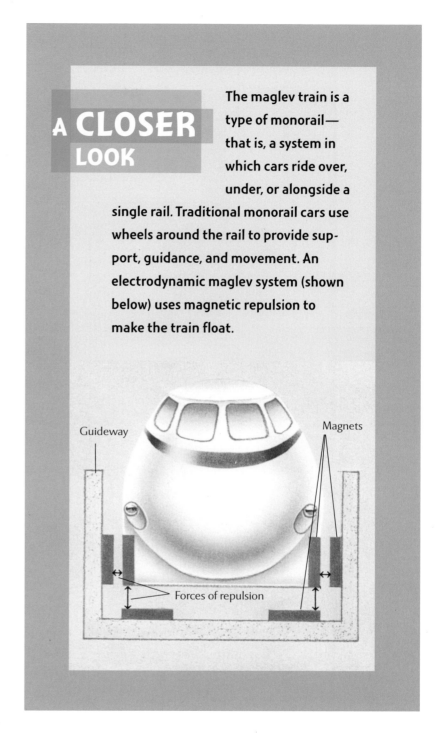

A CLOSER LOOK

The maglev train is a type of monorail—that is, a system in which cars ride over, under, or alongside a single rail. Traditional monorail cars use wheels around the rail to provide support, guidance, and movement. An electrodynamic maglev system (shown below) uses magnetic repulsion to make the train float.

Guideway

Magnets

Forces of repulsion

Today, researchers are developing maglev trains for high-speed travel in Germany, Japan, the United States, and other countries.

► The Space Shuttle

The U.S. space shuttle Atlantis touches down. The drag chute helps slow the shuttle down upon landing.

Long before humans flew in balloons or airplanes, people dreamed of leaving Earth and exploring space. As far back as the early 1600's, the German astronomer Johannes Kepler described what it might be like to travel to other worlds. But it wasn't until 1903 that a Russian teacher named Konstantin Tsiolkovsky completed the first scientific paper on the use of rockets for space travel.

Rocket research took off in the 1930's in Germany, the United States, and the Soviet Union. Serious efforts to design spacecraft picked up in the

1950's. In January 1961, the United States sent a chimpanzee into space. In April of that same year, Yuri Gagarin, a Soviet air force pilot, became the first human to travel into space. He orbited (circled around) Earth once and returned safely. In July 1969, the U.S. astronaut Neil Armstrong became the first person to set foot on the moon.

Early spacecraft returned to Earth by splashdown—that is, by drifting under a parachute and landing in an ocean. After splashdown, the craft and astronauts were picked up by a ship. These splashdowns required many ships and aircraft, and the spacecraft usually could not be used again. There was also the risk that the craft could sink with the astronauts still inside.

In 1972, the United States launched its **space shuttle** project. The project's goal was to design a spacecraft that would blast off like a rocket and land like an airplane. After years of development, the U.S. space shuttle Columbia blasted off in April 1981. It was the first spacecraft able to land on a runway, and thus the first reusable spaceship.

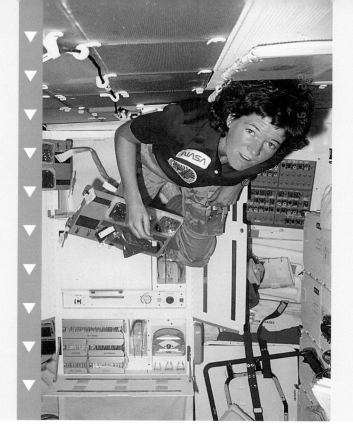

Sally Ride

Sally Kristen Ride (1951-   ) was the first American woman in space. In June 1983, she and four other astronauts made a six-day flight on the space shuttle Challenger. During the flight, Ride helped launch satellites and conduct experiments. She made her second shuttle flight in October 1984.

Ride was born in Los Angeles. In 1978, she was chosen for training to become an astronaut. Ride left the astronaut program in 1987. She went on to teach at Stanford University in California. In 1989, she became a professor at the University of California at San Diego.

Space shuttles can carry **satellites,** space **probes,** and other heavy loads into orbit around Earth. They can also retrieve or repair satellites or **space stations** that need service. The United States has launched more than 100 shuttle missions over the years, including secret missions to put observation satellites in space for military purposes.

The U.S. shuttle program is scheduled to end by 2010. Several organizations are developing technology to replace it. At the same time, many private companies are developing spacecraft in the hopes that space travel will someday be as common as air travel is today.

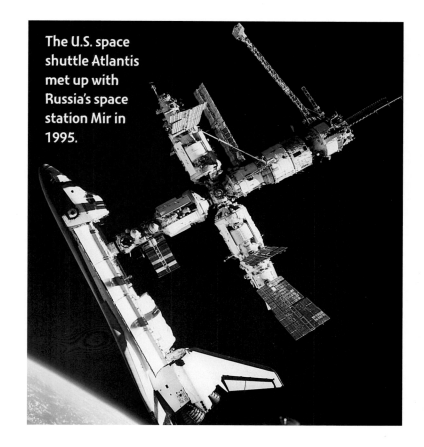

The U.S. space shuttle Atlantis met up with Russia's space station Mir in 1995.

► The Global Positioning System

Computerized GPS devices can provide detailed driving directions.

With the use of radio on ships and airplanes in the early 1900's, the period of electronic navigation began. Over the decades that followed, a number of advancements made navigation easier and more effective. By the end of the 1900's, a worldwide system called the **Global Positioning System (GPS)** was in use. The GPS uses **radio signals** broadcast by **satellites** to help people find their way.

In 1960, the United States Navy launched a satellite called TRANSIT 1B. It was the first step in the development of modern satellite navigation technology. The TRANSIT system had seven satellites and began daily operation in 1964. Soon, the U.S. armed forces began developing a more advanced navigation system.

In the early 1970's, the United States launched the first satellites of the Navstar Global Positioning System. The system became fully operational in 1995. The 24 Navstar satellites broadcast radio signals that are picked up by a computerized radio receiver, commonly called a GPS receiver. The receiver uses the signals broadcast by the satellites to calculate its own position.

The GPS receiver can determine its **latitude** and **longitude** (position on Earth), its altitude (height relative to

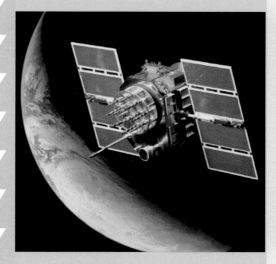

GPS satellites like this one send signals to Earth to help people figure out where they are.

The satellites are in orbit all around the planet, tracking every area of ground and sea.

sea level), its direction of movement, and its speed. GPS users can normally determine their location within 10 meters (33 feet). Some more advanced GPS receivers are accurate to within 1 centimeter (0.4 inch).

The GPS satellites are operated by the U.S. Air Force, and they are used for a variety of military purposes. For instance, they can help coordinate troop movements and guide bombs. But the GPS can also be used by the general public. Hikers and other people on foot may use small, portable GPS receivers. People in boats and aircraft use receivers to navigate the seas and skies all over the world. Many drivers use GPS receivers in

their cars to get turn-by-turn directions to their destinations.

Before the development of GPS, navigation required a fair amount of skill. But with a modern GPS receiver, even beginners can find their way in an unfamiliar area.

Hikers and people on foot can use a small, portable GPS receiver.

▶ The Hybrid Car

Hybrid cars, like this Lexus RX, combine a gasoline-powered engine with a battery-powered electric motor.

People throughout the world rely on the burning of fuel to run the engines of cars, boats, airplanes, and other machines. However, the burning of fuel releases smoke and fumes that cause **pollution.** Pollution harms everything around it: the air, the water, the soil, and people and animals. Scientists believe that pollution also contributes to **global warming** (an increase in the average temperature of Earth's surface), which can have a wide range of damaging effects. With these problems in mind, scientists and **engineers** have sought to reduce the amount of fuel automo-

biles use and the amount of air pollution they cause.

Near the end of the 1900's, the **hybrid car** became available. The word *hybrid* means "a combination of two or more things." In the case of hybrid cars, the vehicles combine an **internal-combustion engine** with a motor powered by an electric battery.

In a hybrid car, the drive shaft, which delivers power to the wheels, may use power from the engine, the electric motor, or both. If a car runs on its gasoline-fueled engine only half the time, it produces much less pollution than a traditional car does.

The invention of the hybrid car is not a new one. Ferdinand Porsche built the first gasoline-electric hybrid car in 1899. Several other hybrids were made in the following years. However, production soon stopped, as gasoline-powered cars had become more powerful and were cheaper to operate.

In the late 1900's, increasing concerns about air pollution and fuel supplies led to renewed interest in hybrid cars. The Toyota Prius was

A hybrid car's gasoline engine powers an alternator, which produces **electric current**. An inverter converts the alternator's alternating current to direct current to be stored in a pack of batteries. The batteries supply electric power to the car's motor as needed. Braking the car charges the batteries. The electric motor can also act as a generator to produce electric power for storage in the batteries.

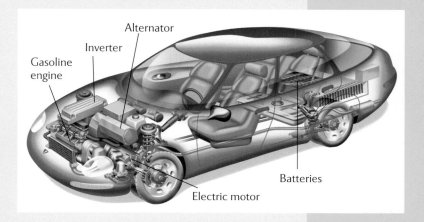

Gasoline engine · Inverter · Alternator · Batteries · Electric motor

the first mass-produced hybrid car. It was first sold in Japan in 1997. In the years that followed, many police cars, taxis, buses, and other public vehicles switched to hybrid engines.

Compared with traditional automobiles, hybrid cars have better fuel economy—that is, they use less gasoline. They also produce less pollution. However, hybrid cars cost more to produce. As the development of hybrid cars progresses, experts believe the cost will go down.

As people become more aware of the environmental effects of automobile travel, researchers continue to develop better engines. At the same time, inventors work to develop new devices that could replace fuel-burning engines altogether.

	Gasoline-powered car	Hybrid car
Fuel source	Gasoline	Gasoline and electricity
Fuel economy in miles per gallon in kilometers per liter	21 8.93	44 18.71
Fuel energy use (in kilojoules per kilometer)	3,282	1,536
Acceleration 0-60 miles per hour (0-97 kilometers per hour)	18 seconds	10 seconds
Engine efficiency (average)	21%	30%
Types of emissions (waste gases) produced	Water vapor, carbon dioxide, carbon monoxide, hydrocarbons, nitrogen oxides	Carbon monoxide*, hydrocarbons*, nitrogen oxides*

*Very small amounts.

Sources: Demirdöven, Nurettin, and John Deutch. "Hybrid Cars Now, Fuel Cell Cars Later." Science, Aug. 13, 2004, pp. 974-976; "Fuel Cells in Transportation." Fuel Cells 2000. http://www.fuelcells.org.

Critically reviewed by Panos Y. Papalambros, Ph.D., Department of Mechanical Engineering, University of Michigan.

Important Dates in Transportation

c. 5000 B.C. People began to use donkeys and oxen as pack animals.

c. 3500 B.C. The Mesopotamians probably built the first wheeled vehicles.

c. 3200 B.C. The Egyptians invented sails and produced the first sailboats.

c. A.D. 100 Chinese and Mediterranean navigators probably first used magnetic compasses to guide their ships.

A.D. 400's The stirrup reached Europe and India from China.

c. A.D. 1200 Shipbuilders in northern Europe introduced the sternpost rudder.

c. 1450 Mediterranean shipbuilders developed the full-rigged sailing ship.

1700's British inventors developed the steam engine.

1807 The first commercially successful steamboat service began in the United States.

1825 The first successful steam railroad began operations in England.

1880's German inventors built gasoline-powered engines that could be used in cars.

1890's French engineers built the first gasoline-powered vehicles with automobile bodies.

1903 Orville and Wilbur Wright of the United States made the world's first flight in a power-driven, heavier-than-air machine.

1920's Automobiles became the chief means of passenger transportation in the United States.

1950's The first commercial jet airliners began service.

1961 Yuri Gagarin of the Soviet Union became the first human to travel into space.

1972 The United States launched its space shuttle project.

1976 The first supersonic passenger airliner, the Concorde, began service between Europe and the United States.

1995 The Navstar Global Positioning System (GPS) became fully operational.

1997 The Toyota Prius, the first mass-produced hybrid automobile, went on sale in Japan.

2004 The first commercial maglev rail system began operations in Shanghai, China.

► Glossary

airship a lighter-than-air aircraft with an engine.

assembly line a row of workers and machines along which work is passed until the final product is made.

BMX bicycle racing on dirt tracks; also called bicycle motocross.

canal a waterway dug across land.

cardinal points the four main directions of the compass: north, south, east, and west.

cargo a load of goods carried by a ship or aircraft.

chain-and-sprocket system a system on a bicycle in which pedal rotations move a chain that causes the rear wheel to turn.

chariot a two-wheeled or four-wheeled vehicle, usually drawn by a horse.

civilization nations and peoples that have reached advanced stages in social development.

compass a device for determining direction.

diesel engine an internal-combustion engine in which fuel oil is ignited by heat from compression of air in the cylinder heads.

draisine a scooterlike vehicle that was the bicycle's first direct ancestor.

electric current the movement or flow of electric charges.

engineer a person who plans and builds engines, machines, roads, bridges, canals, forts, or the like.

free flight flight in a vehicle not tied to the ground.

freight materials or goods transported from one place to another.

friction a rubbing of one object against another. Friction typically creates heat.

glider an aircraft that resembles an airplane but has no engine.

Global Positioning System (GPS) a worldwide navigation system that uses radio signals broadcast by satellites.

global warming an increase in the average temperature of Earth's surface.

high-wheeler a type of early bicycle with a huge front wheel and a small rear wheel.

hybrid car an automobile powered by more than one source of energy.

industry any branch of business, trade, or manufacture.

internal-combustion engine a device in which the burning of a mixture of fuel and air produces mechanical energy to perform useful work.

jet engine an engine driven by the release of a high-pressure stream of gas.

latitude the distance north or south of the equator, measured in degrees.

locomotive a machine that moves trains on railroad tracks. It is sometimes called a railroad engine.

longitude the distance east or west on Earth's surface, measured in degrees from a certain line.

magnetic compass a device for indicating directions along the lines of Earth's magnetic field.

magnetic field the space around a magnet in which its power of attraction is effective.

magnetic levitation train also called *maglev train*. A train that uses magnetic forces to float above a fixed track.

Middle Ages the period in European history between ancient and modern times, from about the A.D. 400's through the 1400's.

monorail a system in which cars ride over, under, or alongside a single rail.

nuclear power power produced by atomic energy.

paddle wheel a wheel with paddles fixed around it.

piston a disk or short cylinder of wood or metal used in an engine.

pollution harm to the natural environment caused by human activity.

probe a rocket, satellite, or other unmanned spacecraft carrying scientific instruments.

propeller a device for producing motion that has blades mounted on a power-driven shaft.

public transportation systems that provide bus, train, or other transportation service for members of the general public.

radio signal information that travels through the air on radio waves.

Roman of or having to do with ancient Rome or its people. The Roman Empire controlled most of Europe and the Middle East from 27 B.C. to A.D. 476.

rotor a rotating blade of a helicopter.

rudder a movable flat piece of wood or metal at the rear end of a boat or ship.

running gear the wheels and axles of an automobile, locomotive, or other vehicle.

satellite a manufactured object that continuously orbits Earth or some other body in space.

sledge a heavy sled or sleigh.

space shuttle a reusable space vehicle for transporting passengers and material.

space station an artificial satellite of Earth designed to be used as an observatory or as a launching site for travel in outer space.

spoke a bar that reaches from the center of a wheel to the rim.

stagecoach a horse-drawn coach once used to carry passengers and mail on a regular route.

starter a device that sets an engine in motion.

steamboat a steam-driven vessel that travels on rivers.

steam engine an engine that is operated by the energy of expanding steam.

stirrup a foot support for a person riding a horse.

suburb a community next to or near a central city.

turbine a device with a rotor turned by a moving fluid, such as water, steam, gas, or wind.

turbofan a variation of the turbojet that uses part of its power to turn a large fan.

turbojet the first type of jet engine used to power an airplane.

Additional Resources

Books:

- *Amazing Leonardo da Vinci Inventions You Can Build Yourself* by Maxine Anderson (Nomad Press VT, 2006).

- *Ancient Transportation* by Michael and Mary B. Woods (Runestone Press, 2000).

- *Great Inventions: The Illustrated Science Encyclopedia* by Peter Harrison, Chris Oxlade, and Stephen Bennington (Southwater Publishing, 2001).

- *Great Inventions of the 20th Century* by Peter Jedicke (Chelsea House Publications, 2007).

- *Leonardo, Beautiful Dreamer* by Robert Byrd (Dutton, 2003).

- *The Railroad* by John R. Matthews (Franklin Watts, 2005).

- *So You Want to Be an Inventor?* by Judith St. George (Philomel Books, 2002).

- *What a Great Idea! Inventions that Changed the World* by Stephen M. Tomecek (Scholastic, 2003).

- *Wheels for the World: Henry Ford, His Company, and a Century of Progress* by Douglas Brinkley (Penguin, 2004).

Web Sites:

- Encyclopedia Smithsonian
  http://www.si.edu/Encyclopedia_SI/Science_and_technology/Transportation_Technology.htm
  The Smithsonian Institute's Encyclopedia offers a brief look at the history of transportation, among other topics.

- Exploring Leonardo - Museum of Science, Boston
  http://www.mos.org/sln/Leonardo
  Focusing on Leonardo da Vinci, this useful site is designed for teachers and students in grades 4-8. It includes a section on the elements of machines and a discussion of perspective.

- Henry Ford
  http://www.invent.org/hall_of_fame/60.html
  Information from the U.S. National Inventors Hall of Fame about pioneering automotive engineer Henry Ford.

- The History of the First Locomotives in America
  http://www.history.rochester.edu/steam/brown/index.html
  A history of railroads and locomotives in the United States.

- Illinois Railroad Museum: Picture Gallery
  http://www.irm.org/gallery
  The Illinois Railroad Museum provides a searchable online exhibit of photos of railroad equipment.

- National Inventors Hall of Fame
  http://www.invent.org/index.asp
  Information on inventions and inventors from the U.S. National Inventors Hall of Fame.

- Women in Transportation
  http://www.fhwa.dot.gov/wit/page1.htm
  This Web site, run by the U.S. Department of Transportation's Federal Highway Administration, provides information about the important role women have played in changing the way people travel.

Index